MW01631361

The Most Important Letter You Will Ever Write

A Guide to Leaving Your Legacy

by Carolyn B. Healy

THE MOST IMPORTANT LETTER YOU WILL EVER WRITE by Carolyn B. Healy

Cover photograph by Carolyn B. Healy

Journal and cover designed by Ellie Searl, Publishista®

Copyright © 2012 by Carolyn B. Healy

All rights reserved.

All material in this book is the sole property of Carolyn B. Healy. Reproduction or retransmission of this document, in whole or in part, in any manner, is prohibited without prior written permission from the copyright holder.

ISBN-13: 978-0988279926
ISBN-10: 0988279924
LCCN: 2012953304

Printed in the USA

Chicago, IL

Acknowledgments

I OWE a debt to Barry Baines, M.D. He is a Minneapolis area physician working in hospice and end-of-life care, who has spent over two decades teaching and encouraging the preparation of ethical wills. His work gives all of us the place to begin our own. See *www.celebrationsoflife.com* for his current work.

Contents

Part One

Why a Legacy Letter?

FOR A LONG WHILE, I thought I invented legacy letters, often called ethical wills, myself. I was a young mother about to leave on a trip to Europe with my husband. This business trip was a rare opportunity, but I found I could not bear the thought of leaving my two young children. My own father had died when I was two years old while away from home, so I was well aware that things did not always go as planned.

UNABLE TO SLEEP ONE NIGHT, I was moved to write a letter to my children, filled with life lessons, what they meant to me, and my hopes for their futures. When it was done, I slept like a baby. How could a simple letter have so much power?

When I got home from the trip safe and sound, I filed the letter away without much thought, until my next trip. Then, I pulled it out and propped it up on my desk just in case. It still had a powerful calming effect.

Curious, I asked around a bit but found no one else who had done such a thing, so figured that I was the only one. Imagine my delight when I later came across the facts: a letter like this had a name—ethical will— and a 3,000-year history, and had application far beyond my just-in-case-something-bad-happens situation. I had stumbled into a long line of people moved for a variety of reasons to leave their imprint.

What is the most important letter of your life?

I CALL IT A LEGACY letter, traditionalists call it an ethical will, others a "what if" letter or a life letter. Whichever term you choose, it is a letter that you write to bring all that you hold most dear, both people and hard-won wisdom, together in one place.

It summarizes your life, your values and beliefs, your history, your hopes, your life lessons. But it does more.

It outlasts you. You place it in the hands of those you care about the most so that even after you are gone, they still have a tangible piece of you to carry with them.

It leaves your legacy. You say how you would like to be remembered, and what you hope your impact has been on your loved ones.

It allows you to extend your reach into the future. You retain the power to comfort and inspire. As long as we live on in the minds of others, we still live.

It allows you to capture the essentials of your life and see how well they match the way you live day to day.

It provides a snapshot of your mind and heart at this moment in your life. It is not autobiography; it does not have to be exhaustive, or exhausting. It is a summary of what you hope people will take from your example and your unique life experiences, at least the way you see it today.

It leaves nothing to chance. You have the opportunity to highlight what you find important in your history and your character.

Where did it come from?

Contrary to my initial impression, historians say that such letters were mentioned in the Old and New Testaments, and even in Shakespeare. This is a durable idea.

Why bother with a letter when you could just call or deliver your message in person?

WHAT IS SAID OUT LOUD vanishes into the ether as soon as it is spoken. Since we remember only a fraction of what is said to us, and memory can distort and change what we do retain, a letter is the sure way to be heard and understood. It can be read and reread, and kept in a special place for years to come to consult whenever comfort or guidance from you is needed. A letter can be clear-headed and unclouded by undue emotion.

When do you write it?

THE SHORT ANSWER IS THAT you write it when it is important to write it. The term ethical will makes it sound like an end-of-life matter that will be revealed at the same time as the Last Will and Testament. But that occasion is only one of many that can inspire reflection and the impulse to leave a trail that others can follow. Transitions like marriage, or the birth of a child, or entry into a new life phase are natural times. A turning point can also come when facing a challenge like a major injury or illness or loss.

ALSO, AS WE GROW OLDER, a new impulse called generativity appears, encouraging us to examine our best thoughts and insights. We suddenly need to summarize our lessons learned, in the hope that others may benefit from them.

These days, some make the preparation of such a document part of a special celebration like a wedding anniversary or a birthday.

Haven't I already made myself clear?

YOU MAY HAVE TRIED, BUT chances are that in the rush of hectic life, your loved ones weren't fully listening, and even if they were, the message fades over time as new events and conversations layer over it.

Even though you may have said a hundred times what you most believe in, you can be sure that you will get more attention on the page. And once you are gone and your loved ones know that they'll never hear your voice again, your words will still be here to cherish.

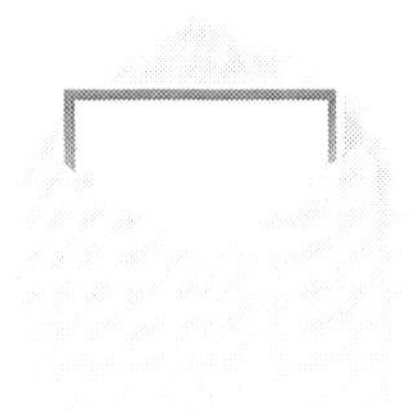

TO WRITE A LEGACY LETTER, you need three things:

First, a desire to share

Second, something to say

Third, attachment to special people

IF YOU HAVE THOSE, THIS guide will help you bring them all together. To prepare your document, you won't need to use everything you write here, but by the end, you will have more than enough to work with.

CAUTION: WRITE FROM THE HEART, not for English class. Don't concern yourself with grammar and sentence structure while you write. Lock your inner censor in the closet and write freely. You will pare it down and polish later.

LIFE UNFOLDS A DAY AT a time. The years collect, and turn into decades. We accumulate life events; we store away memories; we figure things out; we move from one life stage to the next.

One morning we peer into the mirror and barely recognize the face—familiar, but older than we thought—that looks back. Where did all those years go? And what do they add up to?

That moment can happen at thirty, or when the first child is born, or at forty-five, or when the last child goes off to college, or when the first friend dies, or on any random morning.

The past beckons us to review and examine, perhaps for the first time, or perhaps for the hundredth, what is most important about the life we have lived so far.

The first task in creating a legacy letter is to follow this invitation to look back, with new questions in mind about the events and influences that shaped you.

THIS GUIDE WILL PROVIDE THE structure; you will provide the memories, and the wisdom, and the audience.

FIRST, THE guide ASKS YOU to respond to questions about your past. As you respond to each, you may find that the past becomes more accessible and easy to retrieve.

You are generating raw material for your letter, but you are also time-traveling through your life. Prepare for some high points and some low points, and maybe some new insights.

On the practical side, the space below each question is meant to give you a start. If you find you have more to say than the space allows, grab another notebook and continue.

Some of what you write will remain private, for your eyes only, and some will make it into the final letter that you will share with loved ones. Once you reach the last page, you will have put in a lot of time and effort. You will surely want to keep this guide for yourself, as a mini-memoir of sorts.

MEMORY IS IMPERFECT. IT BECOMES bent and distorted as time passes. You will remember what you think happened, and will take meaning from it accordingly. That is the best we can do and not for the public record. If you feel a need to fact-check, ask family members to share their recollections and see how well they match. If they don't, it won't necessarily mean that one of you is wrong, just that you are looking from different vantage points.

Before you write

Research suggests that what we write with pen and paper engages us most fully, so start that way. If you find that too difficult, then open a computer file and get busy.

But don't get too busy too fast. Looking back takes a while, so spend some time to reflect on what you find is worth your time. It will create a deeper experience for you and for your eventual readers.

Remember that no one else can tell this story, and it deserves to be told.

Part Two

Your Beginnings

YOUR EARLY LIFE HOLDS THE first keys to who you have become. To respond to these questions, follow whatever story or event comes to mind when you first read the prompt.

We will start with your family, which, if it is like every other family, was imperfect and probably still is. There is no need to shine it up. Just describe it as it was for you.

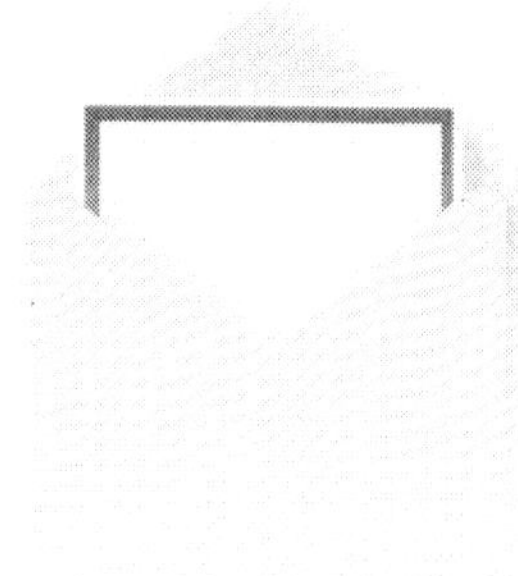

What was the best thing about growing up in your family?

The toughest thing?

Tell a story that reveals what life was like for you then.

How many siblings did you have?
What was your relationship with each?
What did each teach you?
How did your birth order affect you?

If you are an only child, how was that for you?

If your original family had its own motto,
what would it be? Explain.

Were there times when you were embarrassed by your family? Why?

Recall a story that you heard being told over and over as a child.

What does this story reveal about your family?

What did you learn from your father, either from his words or his example?

From your mother?

From each of your grandparents?

*Who was your most influential person
while you were growing up?
Was this a largely positive influence, or negative, or mixed?*

What were your favorite belongings when you were a child? Why?

What did you want to be when you grew up?
Did that change, and why?

What was school like for you?
What was the moment when you realized that you had a special talent or ability?

Tell a funny story from your childhood.

Describe a typical evening in your family.

Did your family take vacations?

What was the first money you ever earned?
What did you do with it?

Did you have chores? What did you learn from them?

Did you have pets? What did you learn from them?

Do you remember any tragedies or hardships?
Did anyone have illness or conditions that affected the family?
How did your family deal with them?

What was your greatest disappointment as a child?

Of the values and beliefs you were taught, are there some that you no longer hold? How did that change happen?

Was your family prosperous, moderately comfortable, struggling financially? How did your family deal with that?

*Take a moment to review what you have written.
Write briefly here about what, if anything,
surprises you about what you wrote.*

Are there any unfinished stories, or more stories that need to be told? Are there any events that need to be included, or more people to recognize?

If so, use the space below to capture them.

Part Three

Your Next Stage

HAVING EXPLORED YOUR ORIGINS, NOW turn your attention to your adulthood, where you shaped your experience and learned to handle what life throws at you.

Take a moment to remember that writing a legacy letter is an act of generosity. Think about the eventual audience for your letter. Unlike a world figure who is moved to write a full-blown autobiography for the public record, you will be writing a special letter meant for certain people in your life. This isn't "To Whom It May Concern." It is "To Those I Care Most About."

Your audience may represent different generations; they may have been present at different times in your life. You may be on good terms with them, or not. You may be in regular contact, or not. You may have unfinished business with them, or not.

Just remember that this is not the place to settle a score. If you do need to sort out issues with someone, that will require a different kind of encounter. It can be just as important, but different.

This is also not the place to reveal secrets like who was adopted, or where Grandma's first husband disappeared off to. Again, that is important, but requires a different type of communication. Do not imbed any other motives here, or it will void your positive intention.

List here the names of the fortunate people who will receive your letter. There may be only one, or there may be many.

Stories

Life unfolds in stories. Depending on how you tell them, they can be brief and to the point, or they can be expansive and detailed. Suit yourself, and if you run out of room here, turn to the Notes pages in this book, or a separate notebook.

It may take some thought to locate which story you wish to tell, so don't be distressed if you do not have one immediately in mind. Think about it as you go through your days. The story will find you.

Tell a story about a time that life taught you a lesson.

Tell a story about a "shining moment" in your life, when you felt the most yourself, the most engaged, the most at peace.

What historical events made the biggest impression on you?

What have been the major turning points in your life?

Which of these were of your own making,
and which were outside of your control?
Was there a difference in how they affected you?

What has your job or profession meant to you?

What is your ethnic background? How has that affected you?

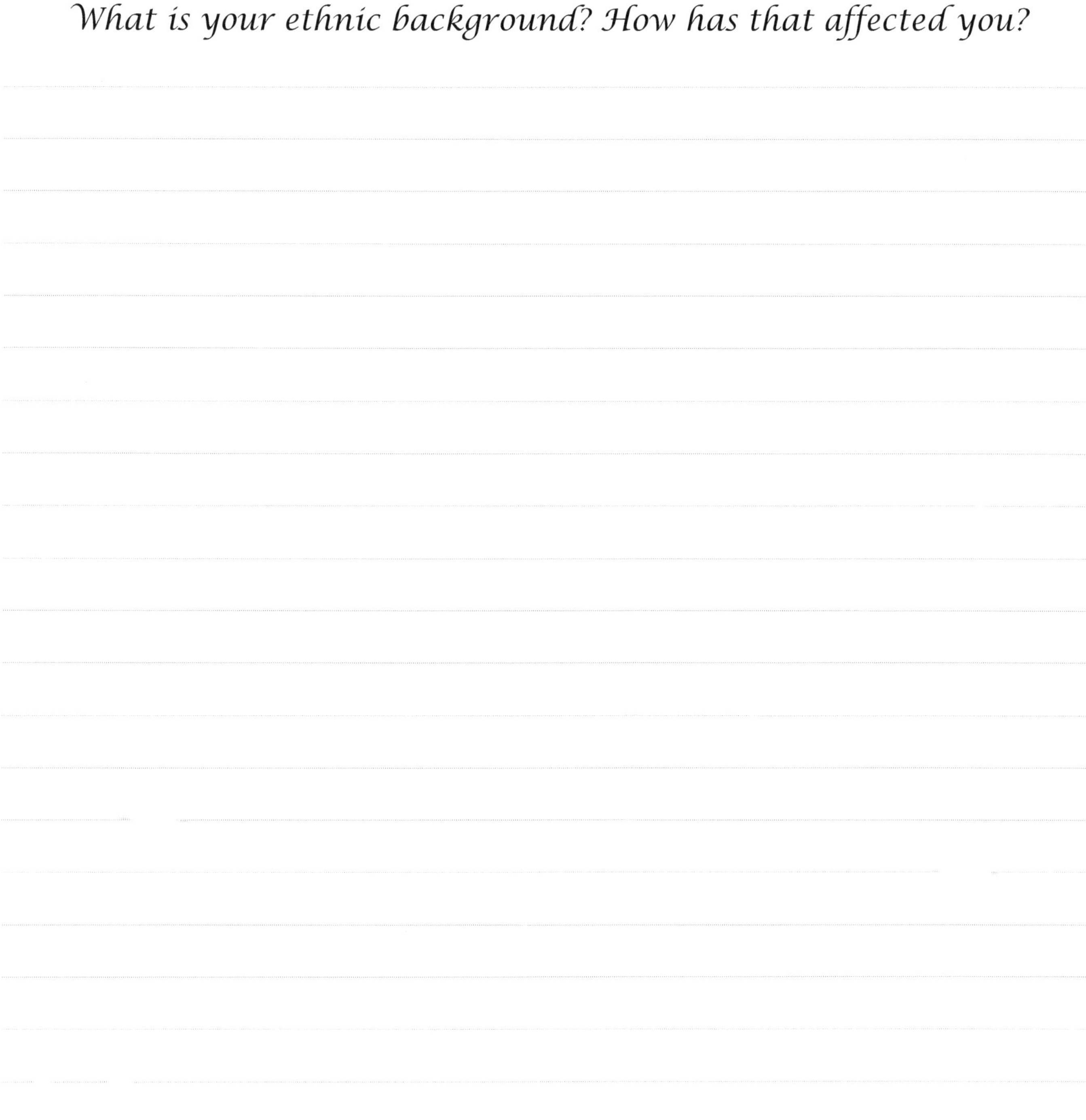

In your marriage or other long term relationships, how did you fall in love, did you stay in love; what did you learn from your partner(s)?

If you remained single, what did you learn from that?

If you are a parent, what has that taught you about yourself and about life?

Have you had important losses in your life?
How have you handled them?

Tell a story about a low point in your life.
How did you survive it, and what did you learn from it?

What is the best gift you ever received? Why?

What do you know now that you wish you had known sooner?

The spot you stand on

FIRST, THERE WAS YOU, YOUR entirely unique self. Then came your experiences and influences. The combination has placed you on a spot where no one else can stand. No one else can speak from this vantage point, only you.

What is a favorite saying or expression of yours? Why?

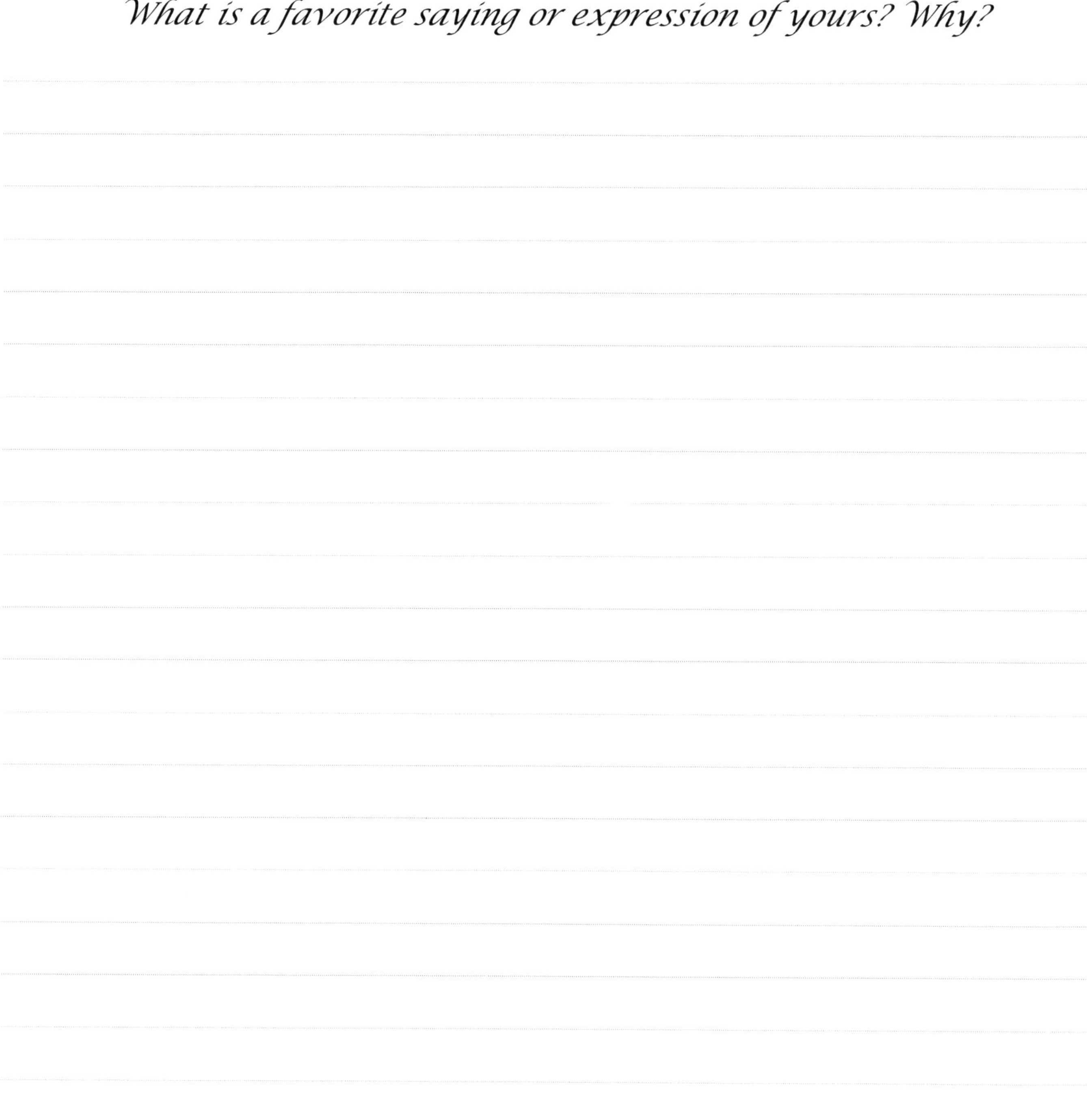

What is your biggest accomplishment?
Was it a solo success or were other people involved?

Has there been a particular cause or issue you have fought for? Why?

What has happened in your life that you never dreamed of?

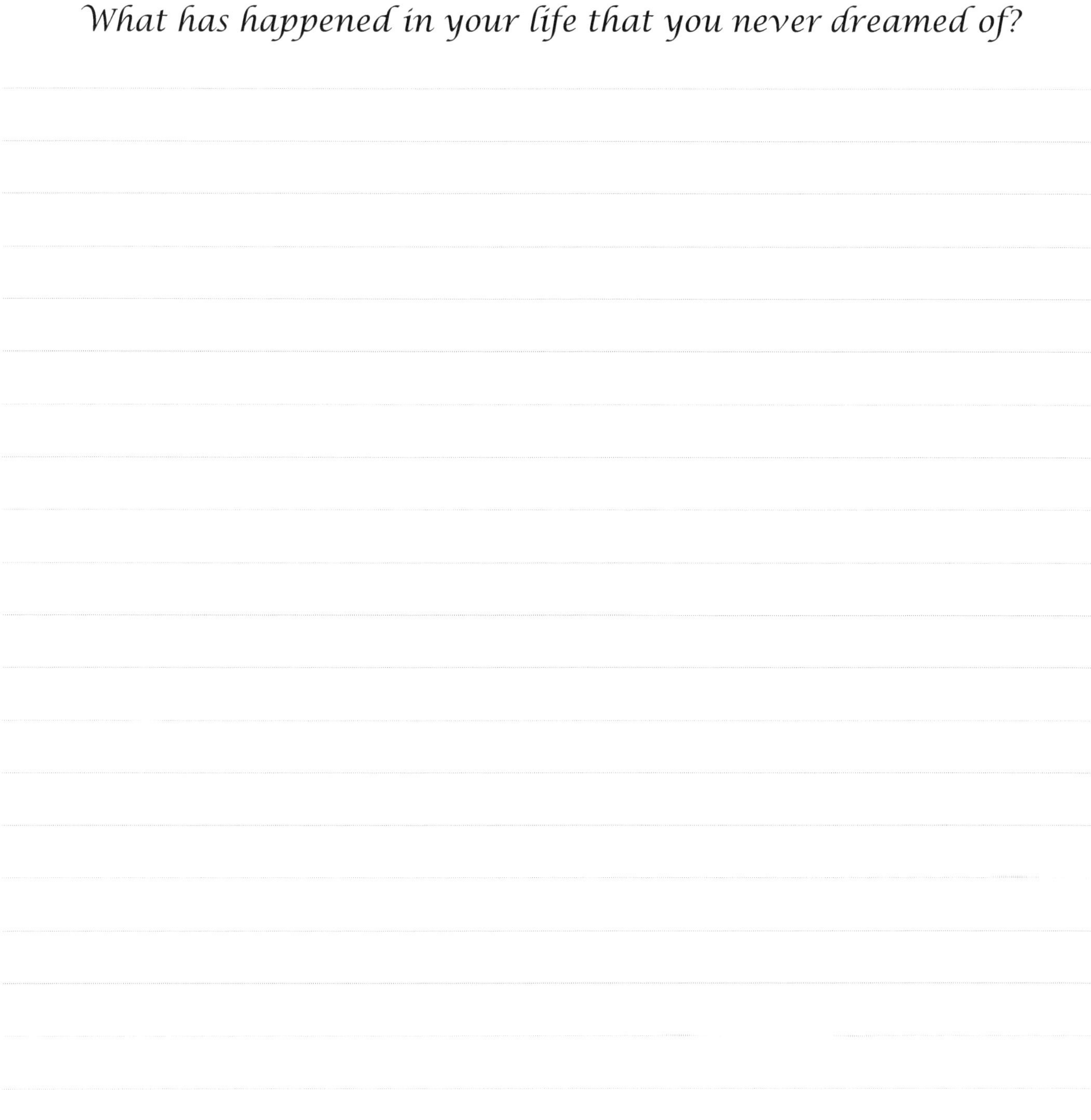

Which home you lived in means the most to you?

What activity or interest causes you to become so engaged that you lose track of time?

Tell a story about a tough decision you had to make.

What did you learn from that experience?

What are you most proud of?

What are you grateful for?

What are your most important values?
How do they relate to how you have lived your life?

Write your memoir in six words.

YOU HAVE COMPLETED A SUMMARY of some of your history, your values, your loved ones, your meaning. Whether your remaining time is short or long, you will continue to grow, adding to the events of your life, and deepening your understanding with each day. If you return to these pages in a year or five years, you certainly will have more to add.

Part Four

A look into the future

NOW IT IS TIME TO extend your reach into the future and leave your legacy. Thinking of your audience, what do you know that can illuminate their path?

Go back to page 55 for the list of people with whom you intend to share the letter you will write.

For each person, write below:

1. *what you have learned from this person and how you learned it*
2. *what you hope he or she has learned from you*
3. *what your hopes are for this person in the future*

Do you have goals or ambitions that you have not completed yet? Do you have a "bucket list"?

Is there a question about your life that you have never found an answer to?

What has been your greatest fear? Worry? Hope?

What has been the greatest challenge of your life?

If people wanted to carry out your legacy, what might they do?

How would you like to be remembered?

As a person who . . .

As a person who was not . . .

As a person who cared about . . .

As person who cared little about . . .

What is the best thing anyone could say about you?

Part Five

Putting it all together

NOW THAT YOU HAVE GATHERED the raw material for your legacy letter, it is time to choose your favorite pieces and assemble them into the document that you will share. Remember, you are the expert here, the only one who knows what belongs.

IN CASE YOU ARE TEMPTED to just hand over this book and call it done, there is a compelling reason not to. You are here to give your best gifts away, but you will want to provide them in a way that your recipients can best receive them. Don't make the people you love wade through pages of musings in hopes that they will get the point. Distill them down yourself. As in all writing, the magic comes from the choices you make as you pare down to the essential.

HERE ARE DECISIONS YOU NEED TO MAKE:

How will you deliver your message?

WILL YOU WRITE ONE LETTER to be shared with all of the people on your list? Or do you want to prepare a special version for each one? Do you want to have one version for each generation? Do you prefer to share the basic document with all, and add a postscript to each person? Or do you imagine recording an audio or video version, so that they can hear or see you say those words yourself? Perhaps you'd like to make a booklet of photographs.

When will you give it to them?

THE OLD TERM "ETHICAL WILL" makes it sound like it must be withheld until after death, a reason why the term "legacy letter" is gaining popularity. It is a personal decision whether to share this document only after you are gone, as comfort and guidance at that tough time, or to share it in a special moment while you are still here. Think it over. You will discover which is right for you.

What format will you use?

IN THIS ERA OF SWIFT technological change, you may want to offer it in several formats. If it won't be read for another 5 or 10 or 40 years, or if you want it to be reread far into the future (and who of us doesn't wish for that?), preserve it in good old-fashioned paper and ink, archival quality. If you choose to record an audio or video, or create a booklet of photographs, preserve them in various formats, and leave a paper transcript too.

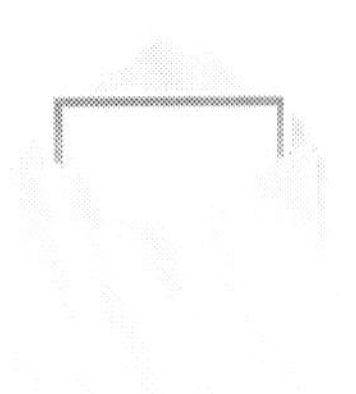

Before you write:

In order to select what you want to include, go back over what you have written with a highlighter in hand. Mark the stories or thoughts or passages that are the most important to you. This will be your content. Think about what helps to get across who you are and how you got that way. Watch for repetition. Don't hit them over the head as much as whisper in their ear.

What is your favorite way to tell this story?

There is no one right way to do this. Your document should fit your personality and preferences, and the kind of relationship you have with your audience. If you are funny, feel free to be funny, or wry if you are wry. If you are the family guru, hold forth. If you have kept your thoughts to yourself, this is your big chance to share more about how you see things. Just don't be sarcastic, or cynical – choose to be your very best self.

How long should it be?

Legacy letters vary from one or two pages to much longer. If yours is lengthy, divide it into sections, so your readers can absorb it in stages.

What is the best structure to use?

THE EASIEST IS TO SIMPLY follow the order of this guide, choosing your favorite content from what you have written and leaving out what is repetitive or less important. This will become the first draft of your letter.

Or, if you want to, you can choose a different structure to match your favorite way to communicate. Examples are:

- a series of stories, or
- a list of bullet points, or top ten lists, or
- a narrative of what you realized when, or
- a list of life lessons
- a once-upon-a-time story that starts with your birth

Or, just start writing and let it come out as it will.

Your Legacy Letter

However you do it, let it be easy. Whatever structure you use, make this letter a heartfelt and cogent message about how you want to be remembered, including what you hope will linger of you, and what you hope your imprint will be on your loved ones. Make clear how they can find ways to carry out your legacy in ways that will honor you and be healing for them.

Draft your letter on the following pages. This may be your final version, or you may want to come back and revise.

My Legacy Letter

My Legacy Letter

My Legacy Letter

My Legacy Letter

My Legacy Letter

ONCE YOU ARE DONE, LET the letter sit overnight, or for a few days. Read it out loud and fill any holes you find.

THEN, IT MAY BE TIME to commit your text to a computer file for ease of revision and storage.

WRITERS OFTEN MAKE SEVERAL FINAL passes through an almost-completed work to be sure it is ready. Make sure that the letter sounds like you and reflects what you mean to say. Make sure you remove any negativity that may have snuck in. Remember, this is how you will be remembered. See if its emotional tone matches your intention. See if there is love in it. And see if you are done.

This is not just a gift for your lucky recipients. It is also for you. The chance to do a life review of this sort can bring you peace of mind. Knowing that you have done the all-too-rare work of examining your life and extracting meaning from it brings clarity of mind and heart. It reminds you what you are about. You will carry that meaning with you from this point on, to guide and inspire you to keep expressing it through your actions.

On from here

YOUR LETTER SERVES AS A snapshot of how you see your life and your impact at the moment that you create it. As time goes by, as you grow and change, this document will want to be updated. My suggestion, based on the many revisions I have made to mine over the years, is simply to amend what you have here when you need to. You can think of as constantly evolving, as you are yourself. Just add the new wisdom to the old.

ONCE YOU ARE DONE, IF you will not be sharing your letter soon, let someone—clergy, spouse, lawyer, estate planner, executor of your will, or other—know that the letter exists, where it is, in what formats, and who is to receive a copy. Think about how to make sure it survives tornado, flood, fire, de-cluttering, and computer crashes. Leave specific directions about what you want done with it, and when.

Take a final moment to think about what you have learned. Now that this project is completed, how do you feel?

IT IS TIME TO BREATHE a sigh of relief. You have left your mark, your memoir, in your own words, to be placed in the hands of your loved ones – the best gift, the guarantee of a well-understood life, and indeed, the most important letter of your life.

Part Six

Notes

Notes

Notes

Notes

Notes

Notes

Notes

Notes

Notes

Notes

Notes

Notes

Notes

Notes

Notes

Notes

Resources

Ethical Wills: Putting Your Values on Paper, 2nd Edition (Life Long Books, 2006) by Barry Baines includes samples of ethical wills, and suggested formats.

If you would like to find a professional to help you write your letter, or expand it into a larger project, the Association of Personal Historians is full of creative people who can help, specialists in memoir, photo, audio, and video versions. Many offer local workshops.

Visit the Association of Personal Historians at *www.personalhistorians.org* (click "Find a personal historian" at the top).

Author

Carolyn B. Healy is a therapist who has specialized in personal narrative and in grief and loss issues. Her website *www.wavesofgrief.com* and blog *www.grief101.com* offer her perspective on optimal grieving.

Other books by Carolyn B. Healy

My Journal, My Voice, a guided journal available at amazon.com. Proceeds go to Our Story Project, a program of Family Shelter Service to benefit domestic abuse survivors.

Our Journal, Our Voices, a journal meant for use by a class, book club, family, group of friends, or to place in a waiting room or other area where people have time on their hands and thoughts to share, also to benefit Our Story Project and available at amazon.com.

As Grief Ebbs and Flows: A Guided Journal provides the opportunity to use writing to heal from grief. Prompts guide the writer to explore thoughts and feelings, and create meaning that deepens the grief experience.

Made in the USA
Charleston, SC
17 December 2012